DATE DUE

This Is What I Want to Be

Veterinarian

Heather Miller

Heinemann Library
Chicago, Illinois

© 2003 Heinemann Library
a division of Reed Elsevier Inc.
Chicago, Illinois

Customer Service 888-454-2279
Visit our website at www.heinemannlibrary.com

Designed by Sue Emerson, Heinemann Library; Page layout by Que-Net Media
Printed and bound in the United States by Lake Book Manufacturing, Inc.
Photo research by Alan Gottlieb

07 06 05 04 03
10 9 8 7 6 5 4 3 2 1

Library of Congress Cataloging-in-Publication Data
Miller, Heather.
    Veterinarian / Heather Miller.
        p. cm. – (This is what I want to be)
Summary: A simple introduction to the equipment, daily duties, training, and other aspects of the job of a veterinarian.
Includes index.
    ISBN 1-4034-0905-6 (HC), 1-4034-3609-6 (Pbk.)
    1. Veterinary medicine–Vocational guidance–Juvenile literature. [1. Veterinarians. 2. Occupations.] I. Title.
    SF756.28 .M55 2003
    636.089'023–dc21

                        2002010296

Acknowledgments
The author and publishers are grateful to the following for permission to reproduce copyright material:
p. 4 Raymond Gehman/Corbis; pp. 5, 16 Tom Stewart/Corbis; p. 6 Angela Hampton; Ecoscene/Corbis; p. 7 Ken Cavanagh/Photo Researchers, Inc.; p. 8 Lynda Richardson/Corbis; p. 9 Larry Williams/Corbis; p. 10 Carolyn A. McKeone; p. 11 John & Eliza Forder/Tony Stone/Getty Images; p. 12 Richard T. Nowitz/Corbis; p. 13 Chicago Zoological Society/The Brookfield Zoo; p. 14 Henry Horenstein/Stock Boston; p. 15 Erik Freeland; p. 17 Michael S. Yamashita/Corbis; p. 18 Raymond Gehman/Cobis; p. 19 Ted Horowitz/Corbis; p. 20 Anthony Reynolds/Cordaiy Photo Library Ltd./Corbis; p. 21 AFP/Corbis; pp. 22BL, 24BL Ken Cavanagh/Photo Researchers, Inc.; pp. 22TL, 24TL Lynda Richardson/Corbis; pp. 22BR, 24BR Larry Williams/Corbis; p. 23 (row 1, L-R) James L. Amos/Corbis, Richard T. Nowitz/Corbis, Siede Preis/Getty Images; (row 2, L-R) David Wrobel/Visuals Unlimited, Courtesy of Cornell College of Veterinary Medicine; (row 3, L-R) Ken Cavanagh/Photo Researchers, Inc., PhotoDisc, Tom Brakefield/Corbis; (row 3, L-R) Jodi Jacobson, Lynda Richardson/Corbis; back cover (L-R) Ken Cavanagh/Photo Researchers, Inc., Jodi Jacobson

Cover photograph by Peter Steiner/Corbis

Every effort has been made to contact copyright holders of any material reproduced in this book. Any omissions will be rectified in subsequent printings if notice is given to the publisher.

Special thanks to our advisory panel for their help in the preparation of this book:

Alice Bethke, Library Consultant
Palo Alto, CA

Eileen Day, Preschool Teacher
Chicago, IL

Kathleen Gilbert,
Second Grade Teacher
Round Rock, TX

Sandra Gilbert,
Library Media Specialist
Fiest Elementary School
Houston, TX

Jan Gobeille, Kindergarten Teacher
Garfield Elementary
Oakland, CA

Angela Leeper,
Educational Consultant
North Carolina Department
of Public Instruction
Wake Forest, NC

> # Some words are shown in bold, **like this.**
> # You can find them in the picture glossary on page 23.

Contents

What Do Veterinarians Do?

Veterinarians care for animals.

They help animals that are sick or hurt.

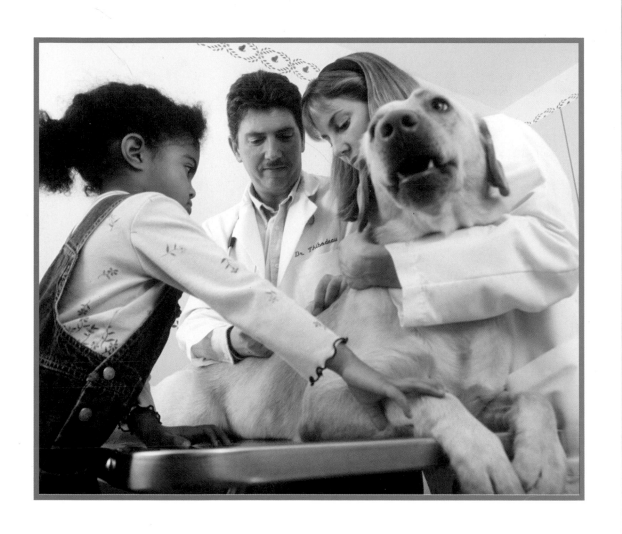

Veterinarians help pets stay healthy.

People call veterinarians "vets"
for short.

What Is a Vet's Day Like?

Vets give animals checkups.

They sometimes give animals **shots**.

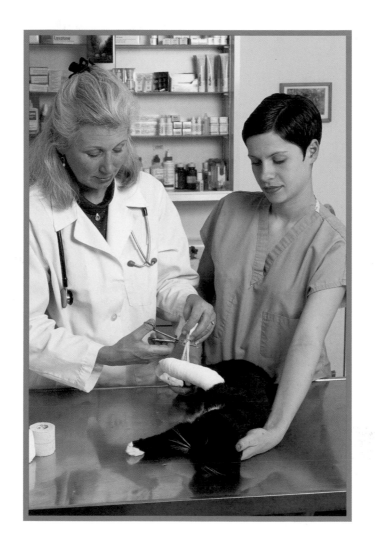

Vets fix broken **bones.**

This vet and her helper are putting a **cast** on a cat.

What Tools Do Vets Use?

Vets weigh animals on **scales**.

This vet is weighing a baby bear.

They use **stethoscopes** to listen to an animal's heart.

Where Do Vets Work?

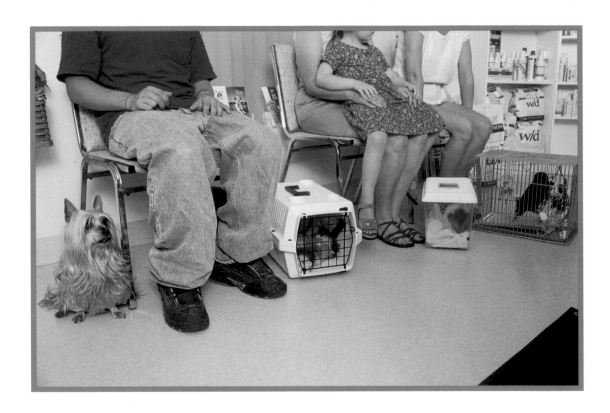

Some vets have their own offices.

Their offices are called **clinics.**

Vets sometimes work on farms.

They help farm animals, like
this cow.

Do Vets Work in Other Places?

Vets work at **aquariums.**

This vet is checking a **dolphin.**

Vets work in zoos.

They help sick animals and care for baby animals.

When Do Vets Work?

Most vets work during the day.

But some animals need help during the night.

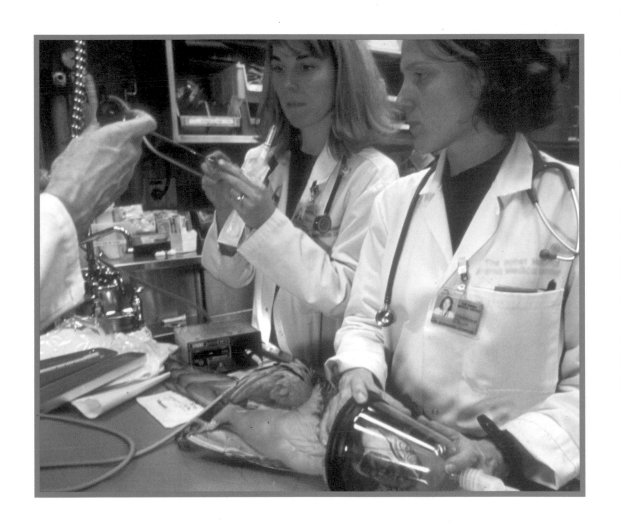

Then, a vet must take care of them.

Vets must always be ready to work.

What Kinds of Vets Are There?

Small-animal vets help pets.

Dogs, cats, birds, and **guinea pigs** are pets.

There are large-animal vets, too.

They help animals like pigs, cows, and horses.

Are There Other Kinds of Vets?

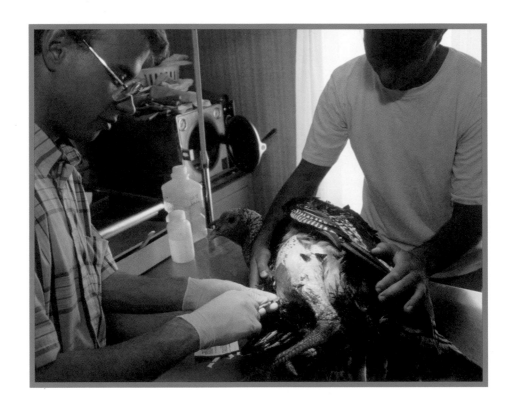

Some vets work with wild animals.

These vets are helping a sick wild **turkey**.

Some vets study animal sicknesses.

They make new **medicine** for
sick animals.

How Do People Become Vets?

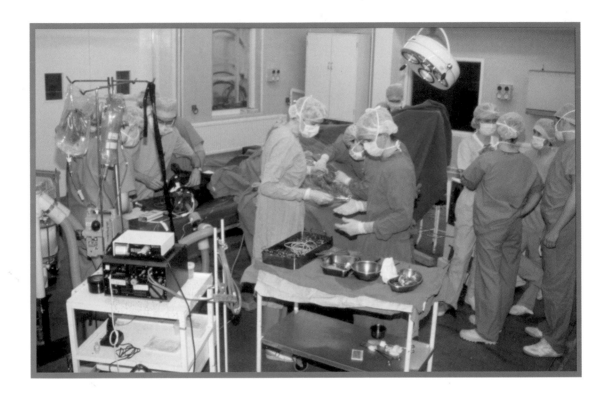

People go to veterinary school to become vets.

They learn from other vets.

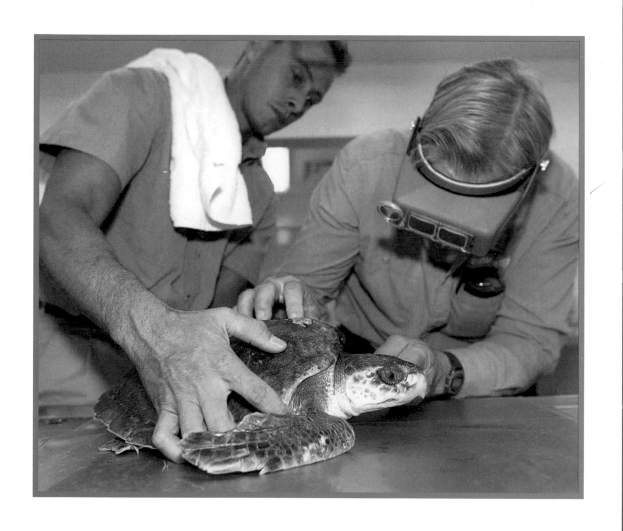

They learn about many kinds
of animals.

Vets are people who love animals.

Quiz

Can you remember what these things are called?

Look for the answers on page 24.

 ?

?

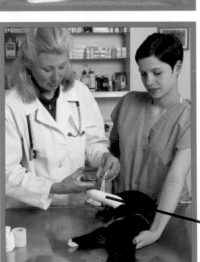

?

Picture Glossary

aquarium
page 12

dolphin
page 12

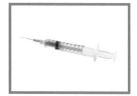

shot
page 6

bone
page 7

guinea pig
page 16

stethoscope
page 9

cast
page 7

medicine
page 19

turkey
page 18

clinic
page 10

scale
page 8

Note to Parents and Teachers

Reading for information is an important part of a child's literacy development. Learning begins with a question about something. Help children think of themselves as investigators and researchers by encouraging their questions about the world around them. Each chapter in this book begins with a question. Read the question together. Look at the pictures. Talk about what you think the answer might be. Then read the text to find out if your predictions were correct. Think of other questions you could ask about the topic, and discuss where you might find the answers. Assist children in using the picture glossary and the index to practice new vocabulary and research skills.

Index

Answers to quiz on page 22

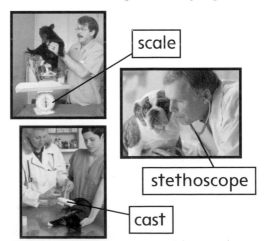

scale

stethoscope

cast